I0459329

invite
PRESS

My Prayer Journal

David Alexander

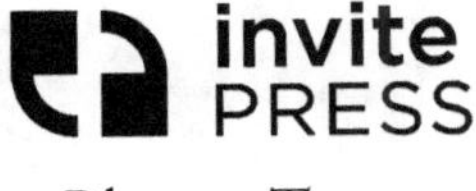

Plano, Texas

MY PRAYER JOURNAL

This book is printed on acid-free, elemental chlorine-free paper.

How to Use

This journal is meant to be a daily tool for your spiritual life. It is designed as something you can reflect on, write in, carry around, and return to, over and over.

Here are the sections:

- Three Simple Rules
- Using Others' Words
- Using Your Own Words
- Listening to God
- Discerning God
- Praying for Others
- Pressing On
- My Time with God
- Appendix of Prayers

Each section includes a short reflection and space to record your prayers, questions, and what you notice along the way.

There's no wrong way to use it—some people write daily, others once a week. What matters is showing up.

Start today.

Write honestly about what's good, what hurts, and where you need help. Record names and needs, and note how God may be speaking through Scripture, circumstances, or quiet moments.

Over time, flip back through earlier pages. Trace the themes and answered prayers. You'll begin to see your own spiritual history taking shape—a record of God's faithfulness in your life.

This prayer journal is an invitation to a deeper relationship with God.

Let every page be a conversation starter between you and the One who listens.

May God bless you on your journey,

David

Introduction

Luke 11:1 says, "One day Jesus was praying in a certain place. When he finished, one of his disciples said to him, 'Lord, teach us to pray. . . .'"

In 2015, YouGov did a British survey of beliefs, finding that 25% of those who described themselves as "non-religious" said that they "take part in some spiritual activity each month—typically prayer."*

Abraham Lincoln, who described himself as a religious man who nevertheless struggled with doubts, once wrote, "I have been driven many

* *Sunday Times*, January 17, 2016.

times upon my knees by the overwhelming conviction that I had nowhere else to go.'"*

To be human is to pray. We each share a desire to find meaning, significance, and value in our lives. We each have hopes, dreams, fears, and anxiety. Prayer is an expression of the universal longing of the soul. It is a normal impulse of the human heart.

My Prayer Journal has been produced with one practical goal in mind: to help you develop and deepen your daily habit of prayer.

For some, prayer may already be a regular practice. For others, you may rate yourself as a beginner. If so, I hope you will be encouraged to hear that even people who pray on a regular basis naturally desire a deeper life of prayer.

---

* This quote was cited by President Obama at the Democratic National Convention, September 2012. It appears to have been first attributed to Abraham Lincoln by Noah Brooks, writing in *Harper's New Monthly Magazine*, vol. 31, 226, published in July 1865 (three months after Lincoln's Death).

"Lord, teach us to pray."

In the Gospels, the best example of that might be the request the disciples share with Jesus at the beginning of Luke chapter 11: "Lord, teach us to pray." We can reasonably assume that these disciples, who had been hand-picked by Jesus, had prayed before. This wasn't some brand-new teaching. Yet, like all of us, they longed for more. Seeing Jesus pray, they asked him to teach them how.

Of equal significance, Jesus did not respond by saying, "You really should have figured this out by now!" Instead, Jesus teaches them because he desires to teach us to pray.

The State of My Soul Today

Take a slow breath. Ask God to meet you here.

What stirs you to pray today?

Write down the date and describe the condition of your soul.

Date	The State of My Soul Today
________	____
________	____
________	____
________	____
________	____

Three Simple Rules

In his book, *How to Pray*, Pete Greig[*] shares three instructions he describes as the best advice he ever received on how to pray.

1. Keep it Simple

We often think that everyone else just instinctively knows how to pray, but there really are no magic words that must be spoken in a particular way.

---

* Pete Greig, *How to Pray: A Simple Guide for Normal People*, (Colorado Springs: NavPress, 2019)

2. Keep it Real

I'm convinced that it's okay to not be okay and that every emotion is welcomed by God in prayer.

He is as ready to hear our hurts as our hallelujahs.

3. Keep it up

We all know relationships are hard. They require constant attention, ongoing investment, and in every relationship, we experience highs and lows. The same is true in our relationship with God. Like the individual knocking on his neighbor's door in the middle of the night, God welcomes and honors our persistence.

My Thoughts, Joys, and Concerns Today

Reflect on your life today.

List at least one person or situation you want to pray for. Note the date and later, any updates.

Date	Joys and Concerns
________	____
________	____
________	____
________	____
________	____
________	____

Using Others' Words

"When you pray, say: 'Father, hallowed be your name, your kingdom come. Give us each day our daily bread. Forgive us our sins, for we also forgive everyone who sins against us. And lead us not into temptation.'" (Luke 11:2-4)

"What do I say?"

If you have a question about prayer, I promise you are not the first person to ask it.

The most common question of them all is, "What do I say?"

This is what makes the response Jesus offers to his disciples in Luke so fascinating. Basically, he tells them, "Say this."

One of the most under-appreciated aspects of deepening your prayer life is that you don't have to use your own words.

A Place to Start

Take a minute right now to set an alarm for noon every day. As a first step, wherever you are, whoever you are with, in whatever circumstance you may find yourself at that time, when that alarm goes off, pause for a moment to say The Lord's Prayer.

A Next Step

Read Luke 11:5-13 for more of Jesus' teaching about prayer. What do you learn about prayer from this passage?

See the Appendix for some examples of prayers we can use.

Using Your Own Words

As powerful as praying others' words can be, we all want to know how to begin to speak our own prayers. Here are three things to consider sharing with God in prayer:

1. Talk about what is good

Talking about what is good is a way of saying "thank you" to God. Even if you are in the middle of a challenging circumstance, when you think about what is good, you might be surprised by how much you have to say.

What are good things in your life today?

Date Good Things

2. Talk about what hurts

The Apostle Peter writes in 1 Peter 5:7, "Cast all your anxiety on him because he cares for you."

Imagine a young child falls and skins their knee, and a parent rushes to their aid. Like that young child, our natural instinct is to cover the wound, and like every good parent, God's response is, "Let me see."

God wants to hear about your hurts. What are some of the hurts you need to share with God right now?

Date	Things that Hurt
______	______________________________
______	______________________________
______	______________________________
______	______________________________
______	______________________________
______	______________________________
______	______________________________
______	______________________________

3. Talk about where you need help

We all need help. None of us has it all figured out. Humility gives us the courage to acknowledge our needs. Whether it be large or small, God invites us to ask for help in whatever need we have.

Where do you need help right now?

Date	Where I Need Help

Listening To God

A Two-Way Street

If the most common question asked about prayer is, "What do I say?" then the other side of that question is, "How do I hear?" It's a question we spend a lot less time considering because of how significantly we wrestle with the first one, but it's no less important to the goal of developing and deepening in the daily habit of prayer.

Like others, you might assume extensive training is required and only a limited number of people have the necessary qualifications to hear from God, but what if we begin with a different set of assumptions?

God is speaking.

Read John 16, verses 7 and 13 and, Romans 8:16. What do these verses say to you about listening to God?

We can hear God

It is often difficult to specifically discern what God may be speaking into our lives. At the same time, it's not nearly as complicated as we make it out to be. The moment one gives their life to Jesus, all necessary "tools" are available.

A good place to begin reflecting on how we can better hear God is to look at the different ways we observe God speaking to his people in the Bible.

Scripture

Read Hebrews 4:12 and 2 Timothy 3:16-17 and reflect on how God speaks to us through Scripture.

The scriptures are a collection of what God has said, as well as a means by which God speaks into our lives and our circumstances today.

Date	How I'm Hearing God Through Scripture

Life Circumstances

In Romans 8:28, the Apostle Paul writes, ". . . in all things God works for the good of those who love him, who have been called according to his purpose."

Notice that Paul is not claiming that God causes difficult circumstances in order to speak into our lives. Rather, the promise shared here is that "in all things," God will never stop working for good in our lives.

Perhaps you have already experienced hearing God more clearly in exceedingly difficult, challenging, and painful seasons of your life. Others might point to moments when they intentionally stepped outside their comfort zones as times when they were especially attuned to God's leading.

How are you hearing God through your life's circumstances? Think of one recent situation that frustrated or surprised you. What could God be forming in you?

Date How I'm Hearing God Through Life

Solitude & Reflection

In Luke 5:16, we read that, "Jesus often withdrew to lonely places and prayed."

One of the common practices of Jesus was to remove himself from others in order to spend time with his heavenly Father. While Jesus would often do this very early in the morning, spending time in solitude and reflection is something we can do at any point during the day.

In our fast-paced world, this can be challenging. We struggle to pause and find focus. One practice that can help quiet our racing thoughts is using a breath prayer, which is a short phrase you slowly repeat to help you find stillness before God.

One example would be to spend a few minutes praying, "speak Lord" as you breathe in and "your servant is listening" as you breathe out.

How are you hearing God through solitude and reflection?

Date	How I'm Hearing God Through Solitude

Counsel of Others

God speaks directly to us through the counsel of others. This requires us to cultivate relationships with other Christians whose wisdom we trust and who have matured in their own attentiveness to God speaking into their own lives.

Hearing another's perspective is a great way for us to test our understanding of how God is leading us and to enable us to receive fresh insight on what we are experiencing along the way.

How are you hearing God through the counsel of others?

Date	How I'm Hearing God Through Others

Obedience

We always want God to show us the whole map, but God rarely reveals the final destination. When we take a first step in faith, God is faithful in leading us in what comes next.

God honors obedience. There will be missteps along the way, but we can trust that the God who walks with us will graciously redirect us when those occur.

God will continue to speak as we move in the direction that we sense he is leading us to go.

How are you hearing God through obedience?

Date	How I'm Hearing God Through Obedience

Discerning God

Jesus says in John 10:27, "My sheep listen to my voice; I know them, and they follow me."

Is that you?

When I speak with a close friend on the phone, I know who I'm talking to because I recognize their voice.

But how does one learn to recognize God's voice?

How can you trust that what you are hearing is what God is saying?

Those are questions worth asking because of our capacity for self-deception.

Here are two principles we can use in our discernment.

1. God always speaks according to God's character and God's will

Shame is the voice of the adversary. Grace is the voice of God.

So, when we feel the nudge to say, "I'm sorry," or to simply offer our help and support to another person, we can trust that nudge.

2. God develops a relationship with you that is personal to you

Psalm 139 is a beautiful declaration of how deeply God knows us.

In the same way we learn to communicate with our closest friends according to the uniqueness of who they are, God does the exact same thing with us.

We should expect that God is going to speak into your life in a way that is particular to you and in another's life in a way that is particular to them. We do ourselves and God a great disservice when we doubt God's voice because our experience may be different from another person's experience.

Date	How I Know It's God

3. But what about God's Will?

In 1 Thessalonians 5:16–18, the Apostle Paul writes, "Rejoice always, pray continually, give thanks in all circumstances; for this is God's will for you in Christ Jesus."

In just a few words, Paul addresses another key question people ask about the practice of prayer.

When we hear that God has a purpose for our lives, it's natural for us to think, "I want to follow that purpose. I want to live in the center of his will for me." Having surrendered our lives, it's appropriate for us to ask, "God, what's your will for my life?"

At times, finding an answer to that question can seem so overwhelming.

Paul says God's will is for you to:

- Rejoice always
- Pray continually
- Give thanks in all circumstances

In our longing for something more specific, this seems too simple. Remember, we want to see the whole map but consider what makes Paul's instructions so powerful.

Everything good in our life really does flow from one of these three practices.

To commit oneself to rejoice always, to pray continually, to give thanks in all circumstances is to place oneself again in the pathway of God's will.

Date	What God Desires For Me

Praying for Others

In Galatians 6:2, the Apostle Paul writes, "carry each other's burdens."

Intercessory prayer is about carrying another's burdens and contending on their behalf by advocating for them before the Father in prayer.

Here are three simple steps to help shape your prayers for others.

HEAR

If you have the chance to speak with the person you want to pray for, you want to begin by hearing their story. An essential question to ask is, "how would you like me to pray for you?"

LISTEN

As you listen to the person you are praying for, listen also to God's response to your prayer.

SPEAK

The prayer that you pray is what bridges the gap between the need that is shared on earth and the response that is shared from heaven. You lift their need to God and ask for his peace, presence, healing, and grace to be received by them through your prayers.

Praying with Others

A significant step forward in becoming a person of prayer happens when you move beyond "I will pray for you" to "can I pray for you right now?"

While that may sound intimidating, there are few things that will enhance your prayer life and richly bless the life of another more than praying with others.

Your prayers do not have to be long or eloquent. Aim for simple and sincere.

Who needs prayer today? Write their name, what you're asking God for, and later note any change you've seen.

Date	Other People I'm Praying For

Pressing On

A final word of warning:

I have found that in any discussion about deepening and developing the habits of our spiritual lives, guilt always lingers in the corner. As I said earlier, I believe shame is the voice of the adversary.

The one I typically refer to as "the adversary" goes by several different names in scripture—the Devil, Satan, the evil one. What's important is the recognition that he is real and constantly seeking to undermine and oppose the work of God's Spirit.

- Where the Spirit of the Lord speaks freedom, the adversary speaks bondage.
- Where the Spirit speaks grace, the adversary speaks condemnation.
- Where the Spirit speaks hope, the adversary speaks despair.
- Where the Spirit speaks love, the adversary speaks doubt.

Remember, prayer is about building relationship with God, and relationships are never easy. As you seek to deepen and develop the daily habit of prayer, here are two things I can guarantee:

1. The Spirit will be working in a powerful way in each step you take

Remember, because Jesus likes you, Jesus desires a deeper relationship with you.

2. The adversary will work to thwart your effort.

A great mentor of mine said, "The only way to fail is to quit."

So keep showing up.

Ask God to protect you from discouragement.

Press on through the days when you struggle.

Savor the days when God feels nearby.

Trust that you are doing better than you think you are.

May he strengthen and empower you as you seek to deepen and develop in the daily habit of sharing life with God.

AMEN

My Time with God

Develop your own "spiritual history."

Turn back to one of your earlier prayers in this book.

What's changed in your heart or circumstances since then?

Use this space to track your growth over time, including highlights from your notes above and overall impressions and experiences.

My most consistent prayer theme this month:

The biggest surprise in how God spoke to me:

Answered Prayers:

Unanswered Prayers:

Where I want to grow next:

APPENDIX

The Lord's Prayer

Our Father, who art in heaven,
hallowed be thy name;
Thy kingdom come;
Thy will be done, on earth as it is in heaven.
Give us this day our daily bread;
And forgive us our trespasses,
As we forgive those who trespass against us;
And lead us not into temptation,
But deliver us from evil.
For thine is the kingdom,
The power, and the glory,
For ever and ever. Amen.

The Wesley Covenant Prayer

I am no longer my own, but thine.
Put me to what thou wilt, rank me with whom thou wilt.
Put me to doing, put me to suffering.
Let me be employed by thee or laid aside for thee,
exalted for thee or brought low for thee.
Let me be full, let me be empty.
Let me have all things, let me have nothing.
I freely and heartily yield all things
to thy pleasure and disposal.
And now, O glorious and blessed God,
Father, Son, and Holy Spirit,
thou art mine, and I am thine. So be it.
And the covenant which I have made on earth,
let it be ratified in heaven. Amen.

The Serenity Prayer

God grant me the serenity to accept the things I cannot change;
Courage to change the things I can;
And wisdom to know the difference."

Living one day at a time;
Enjoying one moment at a time;
Accepting hardships as the pathway to peace;
Taking, as He did, this sinful world as it is, not as I would have it;
Trusting that He will make all things right if I surrender to His Will;
So that I may be reasonably happy in this life and supremely happy with Him forever and ever. Amen.

The Blessing. Numbers 6:24-26

The Lord bless you
and keep you;
the Lord make his face shine on you
and be gracious to you;
the Lord turn his face toward you
and give you peace.